Drama by

CHRIS MATHEWS, JAKE MINTON
and NATHAN ALLEN

Dramatic Publishing Company

Woodstock, Illinois ● Australia ● New Zealand ● South Africa

IMPORTANT BILLING AND CREDIT REQUIREMENTS

"You can smell and taste something new, something passionate, something original, something strong, something fresh, something true and, above all, something young. ... This show is among the very best original theater pieces I've seen in this town. It is a thrilling, riveting celebration of the power of imagination that adults and teens can enjoy, and understand, together. ... *The Sparrow* is a sci-fi high-school story, owing formative debts to the likes of *Carrie* and *Mean Girls* and *Wicked* and the works of Ray Bradbury."
—Chris Jones, *Chicago Tribune.*

"This is a play about finding release from grief and guilt. It's about forgiveness. And it contains moments ... so honest, so genuine they will take your breath away."
—Barbara Vitello, *Daily Herald.*

"Nathan Allen and his co-authors, Chris Mathews and Jake Minton, take a more compassionate view of the adolescent 'outsider' to forge a parable of trial and redemption ... What sets *The Sparrow* apart from previous efforts by this undeniably talented ensemble is the depth of its intellectual dimensions, expressed in multifaceted characters of classical complexity."
—Mary Shen Barnidge, *Windy City Times.*

"*The Sparrow* is a refreshingly strong story told with terrific production values that blends humor, music, drama and telekinetic powers into a thrillingly clever theatre piece. Kudos to The House Theatre of Chicago as they continue to expand their theatrical craftsmanship. Their ensemble gives new meaning to daring collaborative efforts. *The Sparrow* soars!"
—Tom Williams, *Chicago Critic.*

"A fantasy story about acceptance, teenage angst, and the power of being who you are wrapped with telekinetic powers is a fascinating concept to bring to a live stage ... *The Sparrow* presents the best of fresh theatre storytelling. It's original, imaginative, and entertaining."
—Chris Joseph, *Miami New Times.*

The Sparrow premiered on January 13, 2007, at the Viaduct Theatre, produced by The House Theatre of Chicago.

Cast

Emily Book	Carolyn Defrin
Jenny McGrath	Paige Hoffman
Dan Christopher	Cliff Chamberlain
Joyce McGuckin, Evie Sullivan	Kat McDonnell
Albert McGuckin, Jonathan Simpson	Michael E. Smith
Charlie McGuckin, Carol Schott, Elizabeth Gilbert	Sara Hoyer
Driver, Skye Thompson, Mark Gilbert	Patrick Andrews
Principal Skor, Louie Nash	Stephen Taylor
Margaret Rosenthal, Phoebe Marks	Lauren Vitz
Sheriff Rosenthal, Brad Gomer	Johnny Arena
Allison McGrath, Michelle Allen	Lauren McCarthy
Tammy Adams, Shannon Baker	Ele Matelan
Coach Gerald Adams, Stuart Edgerton	Dennis Watkins
Grandmother (voice)	Martha Lavey

Production

Director	Nathan Allen
Choreographer	Tommy Rapley
Composer	Kevin O'Donnell
Sound Design	Michael Griggs
Lighting Design	Ben Wilhelm
Scenic Design	Collette Pollard
Object Design	Tracy Otwell
Magic Design	Dennis Watkins
Technical Director	G. Warren Stiles
Dramaturg	Kelly Kerwin
Production Manager	Dixie Uffelman
Stage Manager	Brian DesGranges

The Sparrow

CHARACTERS

EMILY BOOK: High-school senior, a bookworm. She is weighed down by the past.

MR. (DAN) CHRISTOPHER: Biology teacher at Spring Farm High. He used to be an excellent dancer.

JENNY McGRATH: Junior at Spring Farm High. She is friendly, excited and ambitious.

JOYCE McGUCKIN: Wife and a mother.

ALBERT McGUCKIN: Owns a hardware store.

CHARLIE McGUCKIN: 9-year-old who loves tomahawks and headdresses.

PRINCIPAL JIM SKOR: First a principal, second a … principal …

COACH GERALD ADAMS: Was a great coach—is a great coach.

GRANDMOTHER: Raised Emily for as long as she could take care of her.

DRIVER: Has watched Emily grow up.

ANNOUNCER

TOWNSPEOPLE: All suffered the loss of that day.

    SHERIFF ROSENTHAL

    MARGARET ROSENTHAL

    MARK GILBERT

    ELIZABETH GILBERT

    ALLISON McGRATH

    TAMMY ADAMS

STUDENTS: Including the junior class of Spring Farm High.

    SPARROWS BASKETBALL TEAM

        BRAD GOMER

        JONATHAN SIMPSON

        SKYE THOMPSON

        STUART EDGERTON

        LOUIE NASH

    SPARROWS CHEERLEADERS

        MICHELLE ALLEN

        PHOEBE MARKS

        CAROL SCHOTT

        SHANNON BAKER

        EVIE SULLIVAN

SCENES

ACT I

1. PTA MEETING
2. RIDE HOME
3. WELCOME HOME EMILY
4. McGUCKIN FAMILY DINNER
5. EMILY'S DREAM
6. SPRING FARM HIGH
7. THE HEART IS A MUSCLE
8. LEAVES OF GRASS
9. WALKING HOME 1
10. JENNY & EMILY
11. CHIEF CHARLIE
12. DODGEBALL
13. DETENTION
14. SPIRIT BOX
15. BASKETBALL GAME
16. LOCKER ROOM
17. CHEERLEADER CRISIS
18. THE SPARROW
19. FLYING IN THE FIELD

Intermission.

ACT II

SETTING

The story takes place in various locations throughout the small farm town of Spring Farm, Illinois.

AUTHORS' NOTES

Greetings, and thanks for your interest in *The Sparrow*. This play was a labor of love for its original creators, complete with all of the struggle and strife that great love demands. It was written and rewritten, edited and improved, even as it was being workshopped, rehearsed, previewed and performed during its original 2007 run with The House Theatre of Chicago. We are deeply grateful to all of the original designers, actors and crew who worked so passionately and gave so generously of themselves to make *The Sparrow* fly.

We're honored, now, by the life you will bring to it and hope it serves as a deeply rewarding artistic endeavor for you, your fellow artists and your audience.

We'd like to offer a few notes about our writing style. Because we are often writing and rehearsing, rewriting and re-rehearsing, we use a shorthand with one another and our actors so that we can all more quickly decipher the thoughts and intentions of any given line of dialogue. The shorthand is simple, but it uses punctuation and structure just differently enough that the following might be helpful:

Line Endings. Often, lines of dialogue will flow naturally from the end of one line to the beginning of the next line as they reach the limits set by the margins. But sometimes
Sometimes the line will break early,
before reaching the margin.
Like this.
This is always purposeful
And is meant to indicate a punctuation of thought
Or a small break in the flow of speech while a character searches
sometimes
awkwardly
for the right words.
We've found that these line breaks can be honored and traversed at almost any speed, and are only rarely worthy of an actual pause.

Blank lines. Every now and then, a character's speech is broken up by a blank line, as seen above. This is to indicate a breath (physically, emotionally or intellectually) between thoughts and can be filled as seen fit. On whatever scale, just as with every line of dialogue, something is happening with the character.

Ellipses. Similar to blank lines, at times we have given an ellipsis a line to itself:

…

Whether the characters are rendered speechless, stopped in their tracks, searching for the right thing to say, or holding on to something they can't let go—the ball is in their hands while they figure out what to do with it. Again, it is not to suggest the absence of thought or action—quite the opposite.

We hope these devices give access to the characters and their journeys. They're meant to offer insight. Artists should feel free to use them (or not) insofar as they are helpful. Which brings us to …

Impossible stage directions. We believe in your creativity. There will be some stage directions that are plainly straightforward. Easy: Do them or don't. There are others which hope to suggest landscapes, emotional states or, quite simply, impossible feats to create on a stage. These are open to interpretation and treatment using any theatrical devices you like. Literal adherence might not always be the best way for your company to tell that piece of the story. But tell the story you must, and at a bare minimum, we hope they provide an opportunity for collaboration as you and your fellow artists search for the best way to tell the story to your audience.

Again, our gratitude and best wishes.

PRODUCTION NOTES

The script of *The Sparrow* is full of moments that would be right at home on the pages of a comic book or in the frames of a science fiction movie: a girl with mysterious powers that allow her to levitate objects, spawn explosions and fly; flashbacks to a horrible accident involving a school bus and a train; and, apparently, a musical number?! Among the names and titles offered for comparison in some of *The Sparrow*'s earliest reviews are *Carrie* (the Stephen King horror flick), Ray Bradbury (that science fiction master with limitless imagination) and *Wicked* (the Broadway juggernaut with a budget to match).

And yet, we've seen productions of *The Sparrow* by high-school drama departments that redefined the entire play for us in inspiring ways. A big acknowledgment to the Young Company and Dan Winkler's 2010 production at Chicago's Whitney Young High School—so awesome! Our very first production of the show at The House Theatre of Chicago was built on a shoestring budget and, with the collaboration of our plucky and ingenious designers, composer, choreographer and honest-to-goodness in-house magician, we accomplished every magical moment that we had in mind. In fact, a huge part of the show's appeal, in our opinion, is the surprise and delight that comes to the audience from seeing how each moment of spectacle required by the story is accomplished onstage through theatrical conventions.

By the way, our attitude regarding theatrical conventions is this: be unconventional. And by all means, don't feel the need to be literal in your interpretation of our stage directions (especially the more "impossible" ones). When Emily takes flight, don't feel like you have to strap her into a harness and lift her up on wires. If you've got the means and expertise for that sort of wire work, you may just decide to go for it. But don't forget that the whole town gets to fly for a few moments at the end—that's a lot of rigging. In our production, we decided on a physical metaphor. Dancing meant flying. Every time Emily took flight in the story, the actress playing her would dance across the stage. It helped, of course, that we had a brilliant choreographer on the team and the actress we cast as Emily was already a beautiful and experienced dancer. But what made that particular metaphor really pay off was the moment when all of the townspeople, played by actors of all different body types and levels of movement experience, danced and breathed in unison at the end. We've yet to see another production of the play in which Emily didn't dance across the stage, so feel free to use that metaphor if it works for you. But if you come up with some other way to "fly" that communicates story and resonates emotion, go for it.

Speaking of metaphors, we used a lot of them. We're big fans of any sort of nonliteral design elements as long as they, as noted above, communicate story and resonate emotions. We won't condescend to you by listing the ones we found successful. We've said it in the authors' notes and we'll say it again: We believe in your creativity. So bring all your toys, and play.

One final note on music: We used a lot of original music in our production—for underscoring, for scene transitions and for those moments when people break into flight/dance. Our answer to the impossible stage directions that we gave ourselves almost always involved music, and all of it was written by the amazing composer Kevin O'Donnell. You don't have to use O'Donnell's music for your production, but if you choose to (a choice we highly encourage), then *The Sparrow*'s gorgeous, authoritative and ready-to-order accompaniment CD must be specifically licensed for your production by The Dramatic Publishing Company, Inc.

The Sparrow

ACT I

1. PTA MEETING

AT RISE: *Lights up on the PTA meeting with the TOWNSPEO-PLE, JOYCE and ALBERT McGUCKIN, COACH GERALD ADAMS and MR. DAN CHRISTOPHER. PRINCIPAL JIM SKOR speaks into a microphone, though it is entirely unnec-essary. The TOWNSPEOPLE are scattered throughout the audience, making everyone a part of the meeting.*

ALL. …

SHERIFF ROSENTHAL. How old is she now?

TOWNSPEOPLE. Seventeen.

SHERIFF ROSENTHAL. Right, I know.

I mean, of course she is but—

Is she a senior now, or …

PRINCIPAL SKOR. The sisters at St. Clotilde's have assured us that she's ready for senior level coursework.

ALLISON MCGRATH. Does that mean we have to—

ELIZABETH GILBERT. Do we have a graduation then?

COACH ADAMS. If she's a senior, then it won't be a ghost class.

I'm sorry.

I'm sorry everyone.

I'm not sure what to call them.

PRINCIPAL SKOR. They're the senior class.

And we'll come up with something that feels appropriate for the occasion.

MARK GILBERT. I think we have to go ahead with the memorial service as planned …

MR. CHRISTOPHER. I think we can probably do both, Mark.

PRINCIPAL SKOR. Mr. Christopher has offered to serve as a special counselor in order to make sure we are meeting state standards for her diploma. Dan? *(Offers the microphone to MR. CHRISTOPHER.)*

MR. CHRISTOPHER *(speaks without it)*. Resources being what they are, most of her coursework would fall alongside the junior class. So I'm working out a syllabus that should meet her specific needs. Looking at her Iowa test scores, it's clear she's a bright kid. If she wants to go to college, I think she'll have her pick.

TAMMY ADAMS. How do we know she wants to be here?

PRINCIPAL SKOR. We don't.

We just know that she needs to graduate from a state-certified school to attend college.

St. Clotilde's mentioned that she might be a little anxious about returning. All the more reason, I think, that we should all agree on whether or not we will be able to welcome her back.

ALLISON MCGRATH. Where's she gonna live? Now that her grandmother has passed.

MARGARET ROSENTHAL. She can't live in that old house all alone.

PRINCIPAL SKOR. St. Clotilde's was actually hoping that we could find her a host family.

ALL. …

JOYCE. She can live with us.

PRINCIPAL SKOR. …

That's very—

You're sure?

(JOYCE checks in with her husband ALBERT, who does not necessarily convey any sort of blessing.)

JOYCE. Yes.

PRINCIPAL SKOR. That's very kind of you, Joyce.

Albert.

OK then.

Knowing that there are still several details to work out between St. Clotilde's

And the McGuckins—

MR. CHRISTOPHER. And Emily …

PRINCIPAL SKOR. And Emily.

Of course.

Are we OK with all this?

ALL. …

PRINCIPAL SKOR. Can we take a vote then?

ALL. …

SHERIFF ROSENTHAL. I don't think we need a vote, Jim.

PRINCIPAL SKOR. Well, Margaret has to put something in the minutes.

ALL. …

I vote yes.

Me too.

Aye.

Aye.

Of course.

Yes.

Aye.

Yes.

…

PRINCIPAL SKOR. OK. Well.

Let's bring her home.

2. RIDE HOME

(A car travels along a county road somewhere in Illinois. EMILY BOOK stares out the window next to her as rows of corn pass by. Rows of corn give way to silos. Silos give way to barns. Barns give way to houses. Houses become the small town of Spring Farm, Illinois. The car stops in front of Spring Farm High. The DRIVER puts the car into park and turns off the engine.)

EMILY. I want to go back.

DRIVER. …

Emily—

EMILY. Take me back, please.

I can't

tell them.

I can't be back here.

DRIVER. You're already here, Emily.

EMILY. I don't want to—

DRIVER. Emily, we've done everything that we know how to do for you.

You have to be here.

You have to tell them what you did.

EMILY. …

DRIVER. …

You're carrying more weight than anyone should ever have to carry, Emily.

EMILY. I don't know how to let go of it.

DRIVER. I'm not telling you to let go of it.

It's yours to carry.

EMILY. …

DRIVER. It's time to push you out of the nest, Emily Book.
　　We know you can fly.

　　You just have to do it while you carry the weight.

(EMILY stands and picks up her suitcase.)

DRIVER *(cont'd).* We're all very proud of you.

EMILY. Thanks. *(Opens the door and steps out of the car. Before she closes the door, she speaks.)* Thank you.

3. WELCOME HOME EMILY

(EMILY stands there, face to face with the audience, seemingly paralyzed, both hands clutching her suitcase. The car pulls away behind her. Waiting there behind are TOWNSPEOPLE of mixed ages standing on the front walkway that leads to the steps of the school. As EMILY turns, they cheer and applaud at her arrival. PRINCIPAL SKOR steps forward and offers EMILY a handshake. EMILY sets down her suitcase and obliges as the crowd looks on. PRINCIPAL SKOR and EMILY introduce themselves. They simultaneously reach down to retrieve EMILY's suitcase. The latch snaps open and the suitcase suddenly spills out its contents: dozens of books. They both lurch forward to correct the mess (as if, if they move fast enough, they could prevent what's already happened) and bump heads. They replace all the books into the suitcase, clasping it shut. PRINCIPAL SKOR takes the suitcase up for EMILY It seems heavier in PRINCIPAL SKOR's hands than it did in EMILY's.)

PRINCIPAL SKOR. On behalf of the people of Spring—

(JOYCE steps out of the crowd and approaches EMILY. ALBERT stands with 10-year-old CHARLIE McGUCKIN at his side.)

JOYCE. My goodness, you've gotten so tall!

PRINCIPAL SKOR. Emily, this is Joyce McGuckin.

(EMILY puts out her hand to shake. JOYCE embraces her instead. PRINCIPAL SKOR gives the crowd its cue, and it bursts into applause once more. The TOWNSPEOPLE of Spring Farm introduce themselves as EMILY and the McGUCKIN FAMILY prepare for dinner.)

4. McGUCKIN FAMILY DINNER

(The McGUCKIN's and EMILY are seated for dinner.)

JOYCE. Albert?

   More salad?

EMILY. These are nice plates.

JOYCE. Oh, these?

   Thank you.

EMILY. You're welcome.

   And thank you for putting me up.

   It's really very generous of you.

JOYCE. Well we're just thrilled.

CHARLIE. These are the Christmas plates!

JOYCE. It is like Christmas, isn't it?

   We have a family guest.

   She's brought her luggage with her …

   Her presence is

   like a present

   for us.

   Charlie, eat your soup with a spoon.

   So, Emily,

   do you have any big plans for your first day at Spring Farm High?

EMILY. Um,

> Well, I was just thinking I would go in early and get my schedule and, I'll probably need a map to find all my classes. And get books.

CHARLIE. And then are you leaving?

JOYCE. Charlie!

> Albert has to go to the hardware store about the same time you go to school, sweetie. He can give you a ride if that would be fine.

EMILY. Hardware store?

ALBERT. McGuckin's Hardware Store.

> It's my store.

EMILY. Oh.

> Thank you.

JOYCE. I know first days can always seem daunting,

> But I'm sure you'll fit in
>
> Just like you'd never left.
>
> And Dan Christopher's going to be your counselor?
>
> You'll get along with him. He's a good man. And a good teacher.
>
> You've got nothing to fear.
>
> We're all just so glad you've come home.

CHARLIE. Why?

JOYCE. Why what, Charlie?

CHARLIE. Why is she here?

JOYCE. She lives here now, Charlie.

> Eat your vegetables.

CHARLIE. They're gross!

> I'm sick of corn. Corn makes me throw up.

ALBERT. Charlie!

EMILY. I like the corn.

CHARLIE. Nobody cares!

ALBERT. Sit

In—your—chair

CHARLIE. …

JOYCE. Emil—

EMILY. I'm a little bit tired.

From the trip.

Do you mind if I …

JOYCE. Of course, sweetie.

Your bed is all made up.

EMILY. Thank you. *(Quickly moves toward the hall, then stops.)* Which room is it?

JOYCE. Sara's room.

CHARLIE. Sara's room!

You can't go in there!

ALBERT. It isn't—

It's just a room.

CHARLIE. I'm not allowed to go in there!

JOYCE. Why would you want to go into Sara's room, Charlie honey?

You have your own room.

And it's Emily's room now.

CHARLIE. But that doesn't make any sense!

This house is so—

illogical!

JOYCE. That word doesn't mean what you think it does.

EMILY *(has retrieved her suitcase)*. Which

room is it?

JOYCE. Oh, here let me take that for you.

It's just right up the stairs and to the right here.

Charlie, help your father clear the table.

Don't pay him any mind, sweetie.

He's rambunctious.

You two will be the best of friends soon enough.

And here we are.

Here's your bed.

I hope you still like pink.

The closet and here's the dresser, and mirror.

My,

look at you.

All grown up.

And you have glasses now.

EMILY. I've always had glasses.

JOYCE. Of course you have.

Well, all right, Albert and I are just down the hall if you need anything,

OK, sweetie?

You have a good night and sleep tight.

We're so glad you've come back to us.

EMILY. Mrs. McGuckin.

I'm not Sara.

JOYCE. I—

...

Goodnight. *(Exits.)*

(EMILY switches the bedside lamp, but instead of turning off, it switches to night-light mode. It's one of those rotating gobo lights that casts shooting stars and sparkles around the walls and ceiling of the room. It's accompanied with music box twinkles. EMILY lies on her back, tucked in, motionless, eyes looking around the room. She closes her eyes for sleep.)

5. EMILY'S DREAM

(EMILY dreams about the school bus. She is being picked on by other schoolchildren as she walks down the endless aisle to the front of the bus. They throw things at her and sing songs at her. Something about living on the wrong side of the tracks. Something about living with her GRANDMOTHER. A child reaches into the aisle and grabs EMILY's lunchbox. He throws it out the window.

EMILY steps off the bus and goes to pick up her lunchbox. The kids continue to tease and throw papers at her from inside the bus. EMILY looks to the house. Her GRANDMA stands in the doorway. The railroad crossing lights begin to flash and ring into ...)

6. SPRING FARM HIGH

(The empty halls of Spring Farm High. EMILY hears PRINCIPAL SKOR address the building over the PA system.)

PRINCIPAL SKOR. Good morning, students.

Principal Skor here.

Remember ... if you ever need guidance on your principles,

you can always talk to ... your principal.

(The school bell rings. Spring Farm High bursts into morning bustle. Lockers, girls looking on, boys unadjusted to their recent growth spurts and burgeoning Adam's apples. Varsity jackets and pleated skirts. Some kid has a pocket protector. Teachers with hair buns. Posters advertising the big homecoming basketball game with phrases like "This is the Year!" and "We Believe in Our Team!" EMILY feels like an outsider as the life of the school swirls around her. She arrives at a classroom and a desk.)

7. THE HEART IS A MUSCLE

(EMILY sits surrounded by empty desks. The bell rings. STUDENTS amble into class, some skirting in at the last minute to take their seats simultaneously with the ring of the bell. Upon entering, STUDENTS have been placing home-work on the teacher's desk, some obviously cheating at the last minute. Rustles of books and bookbags, notebooks and leafed pages. Chatter. MR. CHRISTOPHER takes the front, walking to a pull-down chart, which he pulls down. It is a colored diagram of the human heart.)

MR. CHRISTOPHER. The heart!—

Is a muscle.

What type of muscle is it? For 200 of my dollars, M(r/s). ____ —

STUDENT. Involuntary!

MR. CHRISTOPHER. Yes! It's involuntary.

You can't control it.

It works, whether you want it to or not,

you cannot start or stop it on purpose.

In a healthy human body at rest,

the heart will beat 60 to 80 times a minute,

pumping oxygen-carrying blood throughout the body.

Always beating,

always pumping,

always working for you.

Thus, if you were listening, and Mrs. Peterson's English class is teaching you anything about context clues, you would know that that would make the heart a member of which system? Mr. Gomer.

BRAD GOMER. … the Dagobah system?

MR. CHRISTOPHER. F! No.

(JENNY McGRATH's hand goes up.)

MR. CHRISTOPHER *(cont'd)*. Ms. McGrath.

JENNY. The circulatory system.

Along with the blood vessels themselves and the lungs.

The circulatory system is the most basic and essential system necessary for life.

MR. CHRISTOPHER. Very good.

Ms. McGrath hit it on the head—

without the function of the heart there simply can be no life and if there is no life, then there are no singing butterflies to create joy in the ears of bunnies.

If we all did our homework,

then we know that the heart has how many chambers? Mr. Simpson.

JONATHAN SIMPSON. Four!

MR. CHRISTOPHER. Very good.

Ms. Book.

You were not here yesterday and could not have possibly learned this from the assignment I gave the rest of the class;

In a completely unfair and public test of what you know— impress us,

and tell me the two types of chambers in the mammal heart:

EMILY. Oxygenated and de-oxygenated.

MR. CHRISTOPHER. Yehhhsss.

No, she's right, she's right.

Different from amphibians, mammals' hearts keep the oxygen-rich

And the oxygen-poor blood separate, making delivery of oxygen to the rest of the body for cellular respiration enhanced;

I stand impressed.

But I was thinking more along the lines of quiz-worthy vo-cab words …

I'll help you out;

I say atrium, you say …

EMILY. Ventricle.

MR. CHRISTOPHER. Corr-*ect*.

See kids, nothing to fear from the new girl.

So I'd partner up if I was you.

Because—the rumors are true:

Thanks to a generous donation to science from Farmer Yates,

We will be dissecting fetal pigs—

the hearts of porcines are wonderfully bloated models of a mammal heart,

giving us all the opportunity to see big and up-close how our own human hearts function

sans all the nasty ethical issues …

(The bell rings.)

MR. CHRISTOPHER *(cont'd)*. Pages 47 through 63 with questions answered on my desk first thing class tomorrow!

Ms. Book, if you wouldn't mind sticking around for a minute.

Ms. McGrath.

(The STUDENTS leave the classroom. EMILY and JENNY remain.)

8. LEAVES OF GRASS

MR. CHRISTOPHER. Emily, this is Jenny McGrath.

Student body president.

Honor role student.

Captain of the squad.

JENNY. Cheerleading.

    It's nice to meet you.

    Are you having a good first day?

EMILY. Sure.

MR. CHRISTOPHER. Jenny's a great person to know. If you have any questions or problems that you don't want to bring to me, Jenny's your girl.

    I just wanted to take a minute to get you two together.

JENNY. Cool.

    If you need help finding your way around or anything, just let me know, OK?

EMILY. Yeah, "cool."

JENNY. Well,

    Calculus!

    I'll talk to you later, Emily.

    Bye, Mr. Christopher.

MR. CHRISTOPHER. Ms. McGrath.

    (JENNY exits.)

MR. CHRISTOPHER *(cont'd)*. She's great.

    I think you'll like her.

EMILY. She seems

    bright.

MR. CHRISTOPHER. She is.

    How have your classes been today?

EMILY. OK.

MR. CHRISTOPHER. Anything good?

EMILY. We're reading *A Separate Peace* in English.

MR. CHRISTOPHER. That's a good one. I bet you'll like it.

EMILY. I've read it.

MR. CHRISTOPHER. Of course you have.

You like to read?

EMILY. It only seems fitting.

"Emily Book likes to read."

MR. CHRISTOPHER. Well, thank God your name isn't "Emily Hates Biology."

So, this is the list of books Mrs. Peterson was going to have you read,

but you tell me how redundant that's going to be …

A Tale of Two Cities.

EMILY. I've read Dickens.

MR. CHRISTOPHER. You've read Dickens. All of …

Nice.

Catcher in the Rye.

EMILY. Seriously?

MR. CHRISTOPHER. OK.

Dubliners, The Sound and the Fury, Hamlet, 1984, Ethan Frome, Lord of the Flies?

EMILY. Those are good books.

MR. CHRISTOPHER. Wow.

OK, well we can talk about those sometime. *(Suddenly goes to his bag for a book.)* How do you feel about poetry?

EMILY. It's OK.

MR. CHRISTOPHER. Listen.

I can tell that you don't really want to be here.

I get it.

But I want you to know how good it is that you are here.

It's good for all of us.

And I know that you don't need to be here.

Aside from being stuck in classes with juniors, you're

probably smarter than me.

I'd like to promise that this won't be a waste of time for you
and I'll try to make sure you get what you need,

but you're only going to get out of this what you put into it.

And if you don't put anything into it …

It's going to be a long year. For both of us.

EMILY. …

MR. CHRISTOPHER. Whatever it is, you can say it to me.

EMILY. I don't know how to be here.

MR. CHRISTOPHER. OK.

Then that's what we'll work on.

We'll figure it out, OK?

You and me.

The good news is

everyone's ready to like you.

You've just got to give it a little … *(Makes push gesture. Offers her his hand.)*

OK?

(EMILY takes it and they shake hands.)

EMILY. OK.

MR. CHRISTOPHER. OK. Emily Book, Dan Christopher, pleased to meet you.

EMILY. Pleased to meet you, Mr. Christopher.

MR. CHRISTOPHER. How do you feel about poetry, Emily Book?

EMILY. I like poetry.

MR. CHRISTOPHER. You just like it?

EMILY. I love poetry.

MR. CHRISTOPHER. That's what I'm talkin' about.

Leaves of Grass.

Walt Whitman.

Have you read this one?

EMILY. No. I've never read it.

MR. CHRISTOPHER. Well it's great.

I think there's some stuff in here for you. *(Opens the book and hands it to EMILY.)*

EMILY *(reading)*. "I sing the body electric

The armies of those I love engirth me, and I engirth them;"

MR. CHRISTOPHER. "They will not let me off till I go with them, and discorrupt them, and charge them full with the charge of the soul."

Take my copy, I've practically got it memorized.

EMILY *(reading)*. "This book belongs to Jessica."

MR. CHRISTOPHER. My wife's copy.

It's OK, you can borrow it.

EMILY. Thanks.

MR. CHRISTOPHER. You're welcome.

Now get to class.

EMILY. Thank you for …

MR. CHRISTOPHER. New town, new school.

You can be anybody you want to be, Emily. *(Makes push gesture.)*

EMILY. OK.

MR. CHRISTOPHER. I'll see you tomorrow.

EMILY. Bye.

9. WALKING HOME 1

(EMILY walks down the avenues of Spring Farm. She somehow hears snippets of telephone conversations as she passes each home.)

TOWNSPEOPLE. She's walking down my street right now.

Has it really been 10 years?

She's gotten so tall.

I don't know, she looks so strange …

She doesn't seem very happy to be here.

I don't understand why she came back.

Her grandmother died last year, no family to speak of.

I wonder if she's been back there yet.

She must be so scared.

We should just love her, as one of our own.

She is one of our own.

It isn't fair.

I want to talk to her, but I don't know what to say.

Do you think she remembers any of it?

Oh, I hope not.

That's why her grandmother sent her away, isn't it?

Remember her face after it happened, white as a ghost.

10. JENNY & EMILY

(EMILY finds herself back at her old house, the Book house, as it is known. She stares at it, brow knit. JENNY arrives, or was she already there?)

JENNY. Hi.

EMILY. Hi.

…

What are you doing here?

JENNY. I was just—

Sorry.

Nobody else ever comes out here.

EMILY. This is where I used to live.

   …

JENNY. I'm sorry about your grandmother.

EMILY. …

   I'm sorry I was rude to you earlier.

   In Mr. Christopher's class.

JENNY. That's OK, you weren't rude.

EMILY. I was trying to be.

JENNY. It must be hard to be back here.

EMILY. I just—

   I don't know anyone.

JENNY. Everyone knows you.

   That must feel good.

EMILY. …

JENNY. You know me.

EMILY. Thanks for—

   …

JENNY. People are gonna stare at you, Emily.

   You remind them …

   They're all so heavy.

   But you can remind them that there's life …

   You can …

EMILY. Be anybody I want to be?

JENNY. Be what people need you to be.

   You can help them.

EMILY. Is that what you do?

JENNY. I try.

   (EMILY considers this.)

EMILY. Mr. Christopher said I should try and

    Get involved, but—

    I don't know what to do.

JENNY. What did you do at your old school?

EMILY. I read books.

JENNY. Well, you picked the right week to come back.

    We've got the big homecoming game tomorrow, and the dance on Friday …

    You could be a cheerleader!

    Usually you'd have to try out,

    but I'm the captain, so …

EMILY. I'm not really

    cheery.

JENNY. The boys need a bench manager for the game …

EMILY. Like … a towel girl?

    People need me to be the towel girl?

JENNY *(laughing)*. That's not what I meant!

    We could hang out together on the sidelines.

EMILY. …

    OK.

JENNY. Tweet! You're officially involved.

    It'll be fun, I promise.

EMILY. The train's coming.

(And now the warning bells begin to ring. JENNY looks to see which direction it's coming from.)

EMILY *(cont'd)*. Please don't stand there.

JENNY. No, wait, com'mere.

    It feels good.

EMILY. You're too close.

JENNY. Trust me.

 I'll stand next to you.

(Standing as close to the tracks as possible, the train roars past. JENNY introduces EMILY to the feeling of exhilaration she gets by brushing so close to death. EMILY fearfully indulges. The feeling becomes almost too much for EMILY as the train blows its whistle. Flushed, JENNY checks in with EMILY.)

EMILY. Thank you …

 for being nice to me.

11. CHIEF CHARLIE

(EMILY arrives at the McGUCKIN house. CHARLIE guards the door, wearing his Indian chief headdress and brandishing a slingshot.)

CHARLIE. Halt, squaw!

 You trespass!

EMILY *(confused pause)*. Hi, Charlie.

 How was your day?

CHARLIE. …

EMILY. I found this at school.

 Here. *(Presents a shiny marble.)*

CHARLIE. I'll scalp you.

EMILY. Oh, Chief Charlie!

 Wampum,

 to appease your stormy and boastful pride

 that I might be granted safe refuge.

 (CHARLIE takes the marble and examines it. EMILY starts to go inside.)

CHARLIE. What are you doing?

EMILY. Going inside.

CHARLIE. This isn't your house.

EMILY. No. No, it's not.

   …

   You can go into Sara's room

   Any time you like.

CHARLIE. You're not my sister!

(CHARLIE arms his slingshot and fires the marble straight at EMILY's head. Instinctively, EMILY holds up her hand and catches the marble. She is not sure how to proceed.)

CHARLIE *(cont'd)*. How'd you do that?

EMILY.

   …

   I didn't.

   I found it.

(EMILY holds out the marble again. CHARLIE approaches. He looks at the marble. He looks at EMILY and runs away.)

12. DODGEBALL

(EMILY stands alone in a gigantic, empty school gymnasium. She is embarrassed, even by and despite the fact that she's the only one in the room. Hanging in the rafters is an emerald and canary victory banner emblazoned with "GREEN-VIEW HORNETS." Other STUDENTS start trickling in and the gym comes to life with their energy and riggamarucking. There is mention of the big basketball game tonight. Over the PA system.)

PRINCIPAL SKOR. Hello, students,

   Skor here.

Happy homecoming everyone,

big game tonight

against our biggest rival—

the Greenview Hornets!

They've beaten us every year for the past 10 years.

And that victory banner of theirs hangs in our gym to shame us

hangs way up in the rafters there, defying us to tear it down!

But this year, I feel it,

this is our homecoming!

This is the year we *tear that Hornets banner down*!

So let's spell V for Victory!

And P for Sparrows … Pride!

Teachers, back to you.

(COACH ADAMS enters and blows a whistle. The STU-DENTS run in to stand in a forward-facing line at halfcourt. They must be arranged alphabetically, so of course some STUDENTS are nowhere near where they're supposed to be and have to run the length of the basketball court to get to their place. COACH ADAMS, clipboard in hand, starts at the A's and begins to step down the line of STUDENTS, checking them off as they proclaim their presence when he declaims their last names. It doesn't take him long to get to "Book.")

COACH ADAMS. Allen!

MICHELLE ALLEN. Here.

COACH ADAMS. Baker!

SHANNON BAKER. Present.

COACH ADAMS. Book?

EMILY. Here.

COACH ADAMS. Ms. Book, you have a safety strap for those glasses?

EMILY. No.

COACH ADAMS. Safety first. I'ma go get you some rec specs. McGrath.

Lead the warm-up. *(Exits.)*

(The STUDENTS standing in the line look to each other, some T through Y's bending around to see their friends over in the C through F's. JENNY steps out of line and wheels out the ball cart.)

JENNY. Any ideas how we should pass the time?

ALL. DODGEBALL!

JENNY. Everyone know the rules?

ALL. YEAH!

EMILY. No?

JENNY. Two teams.

Each team throws balls at the other team.

SKYE THOMPSON. If you get hit with a ball, you're out!

BRAD GOMER. If you catch the ball, the person who threw it is OUT!

PHOEBE MARKS. You can block a ball with a ball!

CAROL SCHOTT. Once the ball hits the ground, it's dead!

JENNY. Last team standing WINS!

Got it?

EMILY. OK?

JENNY. GO!

(The STUDENTS play with revel. Being nailed in the head is everyone's favorite part of the game. The roughhousing increases to include point-blank throws, shoving and

smacking. Absolutely no one minds, except EMILY, who is nervously trying to avoid the game altogether.

The STUDENTS realize that she's not having any fun, and want badly to indoctrinate her into their ritual. They pick up their balls and prepare to throw them at her all at once. Perhaps JENNY realizes that this particular idea is a bad one and tries to stop everyone just as they all release their balls and TIME STOPS.

EMILY is holding a tense hand out in front of her face, and the dodgeballs all hang midair. In a split second, she resigns, braces herself, removes her glasses and closes her fist. The balls knock her off her feet. COACH ADAMS enters.)

COACH ADAMS. Emily, are you OK?

Detention.

All of you.

Hit the showers.

(COACH ADAMS escorts EMILY from the gym as the STUDENTS shamefully exit.)

JENNY. Emily, I'm—
COACH ADAMS. Ms. McGrath!

(JENNY exits.)

13. DETENTION

(A classroom. MR. CHRISTOPHER is sitting behind a big desk. The STUDENTS sit silently in detention. EMILY enters from the nurse's office.)

MR. CHRISTOPHER. Ms. Book.

How are you?
EMILY. I'm fine.

MR. CHRISTOPHER. Good.

Good, I'm glad.

Do you need something?

EMILY. No.

(EMILY goes and sits in an empty desk near JENNY. Everyone looks at her.)

EMILY *(cont'd)*. I was playing dodgeball, too.

(MR. CHRISTOPHER smiles in spite of himself. JENNY smiles at her.)

PHOEBE MARKS. I'm glad you're OK, Emily.

SKYE THOMPSON. Me too.

EMILY. Thank you.

CAROL SCHOTT. Me too.

JONATHAN SIMPSON. Yeah, me too.

MICHELLE ALLEN. We're all glad she's OK!

We're all glad you're OK, Emily.

JONATHAN SIMPSON. Yeah, but I'm really sorry.

I think I nailed you right in the rear.

(BRAD GOMER snickers.)

EMILY. You have good aim.

(BRAD GOMER guffaws. The other STUDENTS titter.)

JONATHAN SIMPSON. Shut it, Gomer!

MR. CHRISTOPHER. Gentlemen.

BRAD. I'm sorry.

I was just—

I'm sorry too, Emily.

I'm pretty sure I nailed you in the mouth. *(Smirks. More tittering.)*

JENNY. Brad!

EMILY. That's OK, Brad.

It must not have been very hard

because I didn't feel anything.

(A wave of laughs and "oooh's." BRAD GOMER's admiration outweighs his embarrassment. JENNY and EMILY exchange an "Oh, no you didn't/Oh, yes I did" moment.)

MR. CHRISTOPHER. All right, ladies and gentlemen.

As entertaining as you all are

Let's try to remember why we're here.

JENNY. Why are we here?

MR. CHRISTOPHER. The bottom line is you guys were doing something you weren't supposed to be doing and someone got hurt because of it.

BRAD GOMER. You said "bottom line."

MR. CHRISTOPHER. Joke contest's over, Mr. Gomer.

I think you lost.

JENNY. Emily's fine.

We're not as fragile as you think we are.

MR. CHRISTOPHER. We try and protect you for a reason,

I think you know that.

JENNY. Protect us from what?

STUART EDGERTON. Passing trains?

ALL. …

STUART EDGERTON. I'm sorry Mr. Christopher.

MR. CHRISTOPHER. Your parents love you very much.

More than most parents love their children.

Your safety is truly their deepest concern.

I understand everything that you're saying.

I understand how it must feel

and I can see the unfairness of it.

The injustice.

But no one in this town can justify any argument that would allow you to—

when the risks are

unnecessary, it's …

You're paying for someone else's mistake.

I wish I could pay for you.

All of you.

I'm sorry.

EMILY. Life has pain in store for all of us.

The kind of pain that's hard to imagine when we're young.

But it's coming,

it's coming straight for us.

There's no reason to tease it or run towards it.

MR. CHRISTOPHER. What's that from?

EMILY. Nothing.

ALL. …

MR. CHRISTOPHER. No more talking please.

14. SPIRIT BOX

(EMILY arrives at the McGUCKIN home after detention. She enters Sara's room. JOYCE is asleep on her bed.)

EMILY. …

Mrs. McGuckin?

JOYCE. Emily.

I was just—

I must have fallen asleep.

How was your day, swee—?

EMILY. It was good.

Thanks.

How was yours?

JOYCE. Fine.

It was fine.

About the other night, I'm—

I know.

EMILY. Know what?

JOYCE. I know you're not my daughter, Emily Book.

But I've been calling you sweetie

because I want you to feel loved here.

I want you to feel safe

and I want to kiss you on the head and make you feel loved,

even though we don't know each other yet

because I think that you should have a place where you can feel
that way.

And I'm sorry if I …

I come into Sara's room when I feel …

Because I don't want to bring that into the rest of the house.

But this is your room now, Emily, and I won't bring that in here
anymore.

I just … I look at you and I …

I start to think about

what happened.

It's not fair to you, and it's not your fault, but when I look at you
I think about Sara.

I get stuck

I want to be better than that for you,

but I get stuck.

What happened that day?

EMILY. What do you mean?

JOYCE. The field trip—

   You were on the bus just before …

   Do you know anything that

   I don't know.

   I just—Do you remember anything?

EMILY. No.

   I didn't see it happen.

   I don't know anything.

JOYCE. I can't remember what she was wearing that day.

   I helped her get dressed every day,

   But I can't remember what she was wearing that day.

EMILY. Yellow.

   She was wearing yellow.

JOYCE. …

   Thank you.

   Now.

   I have some spirit boxes for the team downstairs

   That aren't going to put themselves together.

   I would love it if you would come down

   And sit with me while I pack up spirit boxes.

   And I can put in the cookies.

   And you can put in the pencils and the stickers.

   And we can talk about school,

   Or boys

   Or anything you like.

   How does that sound, Emily?

EMILY. That sounds great.

JOYCE. Then it's a date.

   I'll meet you in the kitchen.

   Emily, I'm looking forward to getting to know all about you.

15. BASKETBALL GAME

(The Spring Farm High gymnatorium. The SPARROWS CHEERLEADERS sing like hallowed angels. They wear junior varsity cheerleading uniforms out of respect for the senior class.)

CHEERLEADERS. Spring Farm Sparrows,
be good fellows,
fear no sorrow,
Sing our motto:

Fly, Sparrows, Fly!
Our hearts are filled with Spring Farm Sparrow pride!
Fly, Sparrows, Fly!
So spread your wings of crimson, brown and white.

We're strong and we're loud!
We're here to make our school proud!
We are the Spring Farm Sparrows!
Make some noise in the crowd!

We go "CLAP CLAP!"
Sparrows on the attack!
We go "BOOM BOOM!"
Everybody make some room!
We're gonna shake it,
and shake it,
and shake it some more!
Put some sizzle in your step,
and take the ball to the floor!
JUMP!

(The SPARROWS BASKETBALL TEAM makes a dazzling entrance as their CHEERLEADERS bound and flip-flop around them.)

ANNOUNCER. Good evening, everyone out there and welcome to the Spring Farm High School gymnatorium, home of the Spring Farm Sparrows boys basketball team, and boy oh boy, have we got a barn-burner for you tonight! There is not a whole lot in life more thrilling than this annual homecoming matchup against the always ominous Greenview Hornets, who are entering the sixth game of their season undefeated.

And here comes the swarm, pointing their stingers up to that Hornets victory banner to remind us that they intend to win and yet again stow their school standard over the skulls of our students as they have for the last 10 years!

But before we find out if this is the year the Greenview banner comes down, we'll pause for a word from our friends at Dale's Discount Flowers and Shoe Repair.

(COACH ADAMS brings the SPARROWS in for a huddle. EMILY stands with him, fresh towels in hand.)

COACH ADAMS. I'm proud of you boys.

And it doesn't matter what happens out there on the boards tonight, whether we win or lose, we're a family.

We've come here together and we're going to leave here together.

BRAD GOMER. We can win this thing, Coach.

COACH ADAMS. … *(Nods.)*

Let's just have a good, fun game.

Gimme a "Sparrows Fly" on three: one, two, three!

SPARROWS. SPARROWS FLY!

ANNOUNCER. And we are just about ready to begin here as our two squads meet halfcourt for the tip. It's Spring Farm's always popular Skye Thompson going up against the Hornets number 14, Robertson. Here's the tip …

(Whistle. Shoes squeak. The teams play basketball. COACH ADAMS coaches. The CHEERLEADERS cheer. EMILY carries towels. The SPARROWS keep the score very close, and even take the lead at one point. After several plays …)

ANNOUNCER *(cont'd)*. … A foul is called on the play and Coach Adams is not happy!

COACH ADAMS. You call that a foul!?

I'll show you a foul!

ANNOUNCER. And Pete Stilton steps up to the line …

And the Hornets take back the lead.

COACH ADAMS. Book!

We need more dry towels to wipe these boys down!

Look at 'em slippin' around out there!

If they don't get dried off quick, it could cost us the game!

16. LOCKER ROOM

(EMILY walks into the locker room to see JENNY and the CHEERLEADERS in a huddle, talking. She stands there quietly for a second, afraid she's interrupting.)

PHOEBE MARKS. Are you sure you can make that height?

JENNY. If you throw me hard enough.

MICHELLE ALLEN. We'll get you up there.

SHANNON BAKER. And then, once you pull it down,

let's cheer on it!

CHEERLEADERS *(noticing EMILY)*. Pshshhhstthssht!

PHOEBE MARKS. Hey, Emily!

  What are you doing?

EMILY. I'm just here

  to get dry towels so

  we can win the game.

MICHELLE ALLEN. Great.

  Better get them out there.

EMILY. OK.

JENNY. How long were you standing there, Emily?

EMILY. …

JENNY. Emily. How long were you standing there?

EMILY. Don't do it.

  You could really get hurt.

JENNY. Imagine all their faces when we pull it off, Emily.

EMILY. Imagine their faces if you don't.

JENNY. I'm not going to fall.

ALL. …

EMILY. I really don't think it's safe.

  The teachers wouldn't approve.

JENNY. They don't know we're going to do it,

  that's the point.

EMILY. Well maybe they should.

CAROL SCHOTT. Are you going to tell on us?

EMILY. I can't let you do this.

JENNY. Emily, please—

EMILY. …

JENNY. Put her in a locker.

EMILY. No—

  Guys—

  Don't—

EVIE SULLIVAN. Take her clothes so she won't run!

(They strip EMILY to whatever level of clothing would be embarrassing to walk out into public. JENNY, unsure of what to do, watches for adults.)

EMILY. No, please don't.
Jenny!

(They stuff EMILY into a locker full of hanging extra cheerleading supplies. Once done, the CHEERLEADERS bang on the door and leave. JENNY remains, uncertain.)

PHOEBE MARKS. Come on, Jenny!

(JENNY exits the locker room as the SPARROWS enter.)

COACH ADAMS. All right, listen to me now, boys:
You can win this game!

SPARROWS. Yeah!   EMILY. Help!

COACH ADAMS. This is the year, you're the team.
I believe.

EMILY. Coach! Help!

COACH ADAMS. Book? Is that you?
Where are you, girl?

EMILY. I'm in here!
The locker—I'm *in* the locker!

COACH ADAMS. What are you doin' in the locker?
Open this thing up!

SKYE THOMPSON. It's locked!

EMILY. Listen to me!
The girls are going to tear down the banner!

COACH ADAMS. Calm down, Emily.
We'll get you outta there—

EMILY. Coach! Listen!

The cheerleaders are gonna throw Jenny up to the Green-view banner so she can pull it down.

They're gonna throw her up there!

COACH ADAMS. …

She'll break her neck.

We gotta stop 'em!

EMILY. Go!

(COACH ADAMS and the SPARROWS run out of the locker room, leaving EMILY still locked inside.)

17. CHEERLEADER CRISIS

(The CHEERLEADERS rush the court, all smiles and exuberance. They are very good at what they do. They cheer away.)

CHEERLEADERS. The crimson, brown & white

are lookin' for a fight.

You Hornets better BUZZ

'cause we're gonna win tonight!

Shout it, Sparrows!

FLY!

Louder, Sparrows!

FLY!

We're gonna soar and grab that Hornets banner out of the sky!

(They cheer and basket-toss JENNY high into the air. She reaches up, grabs the Hornets banner and yanks at it to pull it down. It sticks—and now JENNY hangs, dangling from the rafters above the court, holding on for dear life. The crowd gasps. The locker bangs. JENNY screams.)

CAROL SCHOTT. Pull it down, Jenny!

JENNY. I can't, it's stuck!

MICHELLE ALLEN. Just let go! We'll catch you!

JENNY. I'm scared!

EMILY *(from inside the locker)*. "PLEASE!!" *(Banging.)*

(Pandemonium. The locker bangs. The metal hinges screech and bend. The door suddenly wrenches, dented inward. BLANG-RAeeeeeNK!!! The locker door flies off its hinges, maybe even splits in half, followed by a flurry of pom-pom streamers. When the streamers clear, EMILY is revealed— standing in the doorway of the locker, still in her underwear. She scans and grabs the only articles of clothing left to her: a Spring Farm varsity cheerleader uniform with a sweater and a pleated two-tone skirt—the only remnants of the locker she's just exploded. Begrudged, she picks them up and runs off.)

18. THE SPARROW

(MR. CHRISTOPHER has taken root at the center of the catastrophe to take charge of the rescue efforts. He erects a ladder and attempts to reach JENNY that way, but he doesn't have nearly enough height.

EMILY enters the gymnasium in the varsity cheerleading uniform. The people in the stands are all on their feet pointing up, shrieking. EMILY looks to where everyone is pointing and sees JENNY still hanging helplessly. JENNY is kicking and screaming, sure she will die.)

EMILY *(rushes to MR. CHRISTOPHER and hands him her glasses)*. Can you hold these?

(EMILY pushes off the ground and flies up to the side of JENNY. She wraps her arms around JENNY.)

EMILY *(cont'd)*. Hold on to me.

(JENNY takes hold of EMILY and together they float safely back down to the ground.)

JENNY *(buried in EMILY's shoulder)*. I'm sorry, I'm so so sorry …

(EMILY and JENNY stand on the floor of the gym, still embracing. JENNY jolts as she realizes what has happened. Everyone stands in awe. The game horn blares. EMILY bolts out of the gym. Still a second behind what has impossibly happened right before their eyes, the crowd follows, amazed and excited by EMILY's incredible, supernatural display. MR. CHRISTOPHER catches up to her first.)

MR. CHRISTOPHER. Emily!

Wait!

HOLD IT!

(EMILY stops.)

MR. CHRISTOPHER *(cont'd)*. Look at me.

(EMILY turns around sheepishly. MR. CHRISTOPHER stares at her until EMILY can't stand it.)

EMILY. What?

MR. CHRISTOPHER. You forgot your glasses.

I'm not dreaming, am I?

You just flew!

You can fly!

EMILY. No … You're not dreaming.

MR. CHRISTOPHER. I know! I never have dreams like this!

How did you—Did you know you could—

You're a hero! You're a superhero!

EMILY. No …

MR. CHRISTOPHER. You just saved Jenny's life!

With super … flying!

You can fly!

That was incredible! *(Laughs.)*

(EMILY can't kiss him, so she turns and runs.)

19. FLYING IN THE FIELD

(EMILY retreats to the cornfields to be safe and alone with her happiness. She flies in elation.)

ACT II

20. SPRING FARM HIGH, PART 2

(Through the empty corridors of Spring Farm High, EMILY hears PRINCIPAL SKOR address the school.)

PRINCIPAL SKOR. Hello, students.

Skor here.

Welcome back to Spring Farm High School,

home of:

THE SPARROW!

(The school bell rings. EMILY is the most popular girl at Spring Farm High. She uses her powers to prevent spills and minor accidents and everyone loves her. JENNY is no longer the most popular girl at school, and is correspondingly ostracized.)

21. PIG DISSECTION

(In MR. CHRISTOPHER's classroom ...)

MR. CHRISTOPHER. PIG HEARTS!

Today's the day you've all been waiting for.

We're gonna slice into these little baby pigs

And figure out how they work.

SHANNON BAKER. I'm going to be sick!

MR. CHRISTOPHER. But do not fear, Ms. Baker.

We're going to do it

with love.

These beautiful little creatures

are here to enrich the understanding and experience of your own life.

To increase our knowledge about the insides of all ourselves.

The insides we can't see.

To make ourselves better.

So, everyone thank your piggy.

Say "Thank you, piggy."

STUDENTS. Thank you, piggy.

MR. CHRISTOPHER. All right, let's get into it.

Remember!

"To dissect" does not mean "to cut up."

It means "to expose to view."

Keep the cutting to a minimum,

your pig is not a smoked ham on a dinner plate.

Good, soft pressure, but you still need to get through those layers of skin. There are a lot of them and they're tough. You've got subcutaneous fat, connective tissue, all sorts of obstacles to get around.

Good work.

Hey, Jack the Ripper, ease up there. *(Takes a scalpel away from EMILY's partner and hands it to EMILY.)*

Sparrow. Here.

Yep, just fish in there and hold it there with your finger, and slice around there and that'll free it up some more. Cut with love. Expose with love.

(As EMILY receives the close attention of MR. CHRISTO-PHER, her pig's heart begins beating. Her partner screams with terror.)

MR. CHRISTOPHER *(cont'd)*. That's never happened before.

(EMILY stares at the pig and tries to make it stop and finally resorts to covering it with her hand. The hearts of nearby pigs begin to pulse as well. STUDENTS scream at the beating pig corpses in front of them.)

MR. CHRISTOPHER *(cont'd)*. Emily, are you doing that?

EMILY. Yeah.

ALL. Cool!

MR. CHRISTOPHER. Well, I'll be.

 That's great!

 Let's take advantage, ladies and gentlemen.

 This is the way it works.

 These are almost exact representations of your own hearts, folks.

 Look at them beating!

 Emily,

 This is great. I love it!

 What else can we do with these little guys?

(Music plays from the PA system. MR. CHRISTOPHER is puppeted through a big song and dance number. Under EMILY's power, he lip syncs to Frank Sinatra's version of "I've Got the World on a String" [or some similarly up tempo and joyous pop tune].

The pigs come to life with the backup vocals. MR. CHRISTOPHER dances his way across the tops of the desks as EMILY and the students join in. As the Broadway-style song and dance reaches its final bring-down-the-house vocal, MR. CHRISTOPHER dips EMILY. Their eyes lock.

JENNY is appalled. The bell rings, and the spell is broken. Everyone shakes it off. MR. CHRISTOPHER drops EMILY.)

MR. CHRISTOPHER *(cont'd)*. OK.

 Good class, everyone.

ALL. …

STUART EDGERTON. Homework?

MR. CHRISTOPHER. Get out!

Ms. Book, can we chat for a minute?

22. HELD AFTER CLASS

MR. CHRISTOPHER *(cont'd)*. Those were some slick moves there, Ginger Rogers.

EMILY. I'm so sorry.

MR. CHRISTOPHER. We haven't had that much excitement since Louie Nash's presentation on the fallopian tube.

You all right?

(EMILY says something with her face buried in her hands. "ermbursed … ")

MR. CHRISTOPHER *(cont'd)*. I heard "reimbursed."

EMILY. I'm embarrassed.

Mr. Christopher, I didn't mean to—

I didn't mean for that to happen.

MR. CHRISTOPHER. Can you not control it?

EMILY. No, I can control it.

I'm in control. It does what I

tell it to do, I just …

Sometimes

if I get overwhelmed or over

excited,

it can get a little …

MR. CHRISTOPHER. Out of control?

EMILY. Unmanageable.

MR. CHRISTOPHER. And just now in class …

EMILY. I got excited. *(Slaps her forehead.)*

MR. CHRISTOPHER. OK.

    The first thing I want to tell you, Emily, is that I think you're
    wonderful.

    Absolutely.

    Completely apart from the fact that you have

    astonishing magical powers,

    you're smart, and funny …

    you're pretty.

    You're dark and mysterious in a kind of…

    Well I just think you're the cat's pajamas.

    You're a catch.

    But I'm not the guy that you should be …

EMILY. I know.

    It's just that it's not easy to be here.

    But you—

MR. CHRISTOPHER. Emily …

EMILY. Everybody looks at me like

    I'm a—

MR. CHRISTOPHER. A super hero?

EMILY. But you understand and

    you make me feel normal

    and special at the same time.

    I feel like I can just be myself with you

    and like I belong here.

MR. CHRISTOPHER. I'm glad about that, Emily.

    I put a lot of thought into trying to be

    that cool teacher, you know?

    I mean, hey—I remember when I was your age…

    Mrs. Durkin? Freshman economics teacher?—I mean, she—

    Whatever.

The point is, it's OK to acknowledge what you're feeling.

There's nothing wrong with feeling … things.

It's just a matter of what you do with it.

We, all of us, just have to be responsible with our feelings.

We have to stay in control.

Tell me you're going to the dance tonight.

EMILY. I don't know.

MR. CHRISTOPHER. Of course you are.

You're gonna cut some rug, slow dance with a boy—

You know … a cute boy, without a receding hairline.

And have some fun.

We'll leave the dancing on the dance floor

and the biology in my classroom

and we'll be all set.

EMILY. I'm sorry.

MR. CHRISTOPHER. Stop apologizing, Emily.

You're late for history.

EMILY. Thanks, Mr. Christopher.

MR. CHRISTOPHER. High five.

Now get outta here, supergirl.

(EMILY exits. MR. CHRISTOPHER looks after her.)

23. CORSAGE

(EMILY is alone in her room, reading. ALBERT enters with a corsage in a box.)

ALBERT. …

Hi.

EMILY. Hi.

ALBERT. You're reading.

   I'll just …

   …

   What are you reading?

EMILY. Just

   Poetry.

ALBERT. Oh.

   …

   How is it?

EMILY. It's OK.

ALBERT. That's good.

EMILY. What is that?

ALBERT. That's for you.

   That's a—

   Here.

   That's a corsage.

   It's, uh, it's for your wrist.

   I thought you could …

   If you wanted to wear it

   tonight, for the dance,

   that's what we used to …

   If it's not too corny.

EMILY. I'm not going to the dance.

ALBERT. Oh.

   OK.

EMILY. Thanks for the …

   It's beautiful.

ALBERT. …

   Listen.

   Emily.

I'm glad you're here and…

…

I'm glad you're here and I hope you feel like you're home because

…

I feel like you're home.

EMILY. …

ALBERT. I'm glad you're home.

I didn't think I'd feel like that

so I haven't been very …

But I …

You make this feel like home.

OK.

EMILY. Thank you.

Thank you for the corsage.

ALBERT. You know, you oughta put on a dress and

go down there and just

have a good time and

dance with everybody and—

It's the homecoming dance, you know?

And you're home …

So …

How's that poetry?

EMILY. …

ALBERT. And Margaret Rosenthal talked me through that corsage deal.

And if you don't use it,

I'll hear about it.

And Joyce was hoping you'd get your picture taken

in a dress and

that's a picture I'd like to have in the house.

EMILY. OK.

ALBERT. OK.

I'll drive you.

Just let me know when you're ready and

I'll be glad to drive you down there.

And if it's no fun, I'll come pick you up.

I'll see you in a minute.

24. HOMECOMING DANCE

(A fast, fun group dance, during which MR. CHRISTO-PHER enters and exits, EMILY enters and is celebrated by the other STUDENTS and JENNY, once again removed from the spotlight, exits in the direction of MR. CHRISTOPHER.

A slow dance. EMILY is dancing with BRAD GOMER. LOU-IE NASH looks for the courage to approach MICHELLE ALLEN, but is interrupted by PHOEBE MARKS.)

PHOEBE MARKS. Louie Nash,

will you dance with me?

LOUIE NASH. No.

(LOUIE NASH dances with MICHELLE ALLEN. EMILY whispers in BRAD GOMER's ear, then steps aside. He asks PHOEBE MARKS to dance. EMILY exits.)

25. SLOW DANCE

(MR. CHRISTOPHER works alone in his classroom, wearing his best suit. Slow dance music can be heard coming from down the hall. JENNY enters in her homecoming dress.)

JENNY. Mr. Christopher?

MR. CHRISTOPHER. Ms. McGrath.

How's it going in there?

Did Emily ever show up?

JENNY. The Sparrow?

Oh, she's here.

MR. CHRISTOPHER. Great.

Everyone's having fun?

JENNY. I think everyone's hoping for an encore performance from you.

Those were some pretty slick moves today, Gene Kelly.

MR. CHRISTOPHER. Thank you very much, but I think my dancing days are over.

Those were Emily's moves.

And my joints hurt.

Why am I Gene Kelly and not Fred Astaire?

JENNY. Because that would make her Ginger Rogers.

And because your neck's too thick.

MR. CHRISTOPHER. That's kind of you.

Have you talked to her?

JENNY. No.

MR. CHRISTOPHER. She's got a lot of stuff going on.

She could use a real friend, Jenny.

JENNY. She's the most popular girl in school.

MR. CHRISTOPHER. …

She saved your life, kid.

It's OK that she's in the spotlight right now.

JENNY. I don't need to be in the spotlight.

MR. CHRISTOPHER. That's not what I said.

JENNY. Is that what you think?

I don't care if I'm not the hero.

(MR. CHRISTOPHER turns on the overhead projector and puts JENNY in the spotlight.)

MR. CHRISTOPHER. Jenny McGrath.

  Student body president.

  Honor role student.

  Captain, my captain.

  You are my hero.

JENNY. …

  OK. *(Embarrassed.)*

MR. CHRISTOPHER. Do that again.

JENNY. What?

MR. CHRISTOPHER. Sorry.

  You just looked like my—

  You looked like

  someone.

  …

  Oh, joints …

  Can I …

  Yes.

  Dance with me.

JENNY. What?

MR. CHRISTOPHER. May I have this dance?

  (They dance.)

JENNY. You must miss her.

MR. CHRISTOPHER. It's OK.

  Tonight's OK.

  (JENNY kisses MR. CHRISTOPHER. They kiss. EMILY discovers them. The overhead projector explodes and cuts JENNY across the face. EMILY runs out of the room.)

MR. CHRISTOPHER *(cont'd).* Emily! *(Moves toward the door.)*

JENNY. Dan!

Stay with me.

(MR. CHRISTOPHER chases after EMILY.)

26. WALKING HOME 2

(EMILY runs through the neighborhood, angry, helpless. She is unable to suppress her ability to overhear the feelings of the TOWNSPEOPLE as she passes them by.)

ALL. The way she caught Jenny McGrath like that!

So beautiful.

What was that McGrath girl trying to prove?

She's usually such a good girl.

Thank God Emily was there to save her.

Save us all.

I wonder who she danced with?

I wonder if she kissed anyone.

Is she going home so soon?

I hope none of our boys tried anything stupid.

Emily could handle him, that's for sure.

Knock his lights out.

The Sparrow.

Who knows what would have happened if she hadn't been there?

She was spared that day for a reason.

27. CHIEF CHARLIE ATTACKS

(EMILY arrives just short of the McGUCKIN home. She is struck in the face by a marble and falls down. It hurts her a lot.

CHARLIE wields his slingshot like a hatchet and shouts with fury as he charges EMILY, ready to attack.

EMILY throws out a defensive hand, and CHARLIE is frozen in his tracks. EMILY spreads her hand open. CHARLIE is splayed open where he stands, his feet barely touching the ground. MR. CHRISTOPHER approaches.)

MR. CHRISTOPHER. Emily.

28. ON THE PORCH

(EMILY drops CHARLIE. He gasps for breath. MR. CHRISTOPHER sees him.)

MR. CHRISTOPHER *(cont'd).* Is he OK?

(CHARLIE runs offstage.)

EMILY. What are you doing here?
MR. CHRISTOPHER. I don't know.
   That wasn't supposed to happen.
   Jenny was feeling …
   She came in there
   and I was trying to …
   She needed someone.
   She needed me to be
   there.
   And she looked at me like
   she …
   I said all those things to you today about
   being responsible
   and being in control.
   I believe those things I said
   and I didn't
   think that was going to happen
   but I let it happen.

I could see how it

...

I could see how it was about to go

and I let it go.

How does that happen?

When you see it coming

and you know you're about to hurt someone

and you let it happen?

EMILY. I don't know.

MR. CHRISTOPHER. I know I hurt you too, Emily,

But I'm glad you were there.

I don't know what else—

EMILY. Is Jenny's face OK?

MR. CHRISTOPHER. What?

EMILY. Did I hurt her?

MR. CHRISTOPHER. I don't

No.

You didn't hurt her.

EMILY. What are you going to do?

MR. CHRISTOPHER. ...

I should tell someone.

It was my fault.

I should stay here and—

I have a responsibility to ...

...

I'm a good person.

I should tell everyone.

EMILY. Who are you going to tell first?

MR. CHRISTOPHER. ...

I wish I could tell my wife.

EMILY. Why can't you?

MR. CHRISTOPHER. …

EMILY. You should tell her.

MR. CHRISTOPHER. My wife is dead, Emily.

I thought you

remembered that.

EMILY. What do you mean?

MR. CHRISTOPHER. My wife was driving the bus.

(EMILY reacts as if the train is coming.)

MR. CHRISTOPHER *(cont'd)*. I'm sorry.

I thought you—

(EMILY forces a suppression of all that she is feeling. EMILY regains her composure and stares catatonic.)

MR. CHRISTOPHER *(cont'd)*. Are you OK?

EMILY. I'm in control. *(Exits.)*

(MR. CHRISTOPHER exits.)

29. TEARS

(EMILY retreats into Sara's room and looks around at the little girl's things, so well preserved for her, by her. She suffocates her desire to cry, causing thunder to roll in and rain to fall. In a decided effort of concentration, EMILY flies her books in a flock of sparrows across the sky of the bedroom. She tries to maintain the only, and most important control she might have left.)

30. THE BOOK HOUSE

(JENNY finds herself at the edge of the railroad tracks. A train passes. She braves standing as close to the passing cars as is unsafe. The train is gone. As JENNY staggers back from her delirium, she sees, staring at her from the distance, plain as it ever has been, the old Book House.)

31. THE ACCIDENT

(JENNY considers a dark possibility. Feeling the cut on her cheek, JENNY sees the bus accident as it happened from EMILY's point of view: the children picking on EMILY and chanting, "Emily Book lives in a shack on the ugly side of the railroad track!" The train is approaching; the warning bell; EMILY's GRANDMOTHER screaming at her from the doorway; EMILY is overwhelmed. the school bus is pushed onto the tracks; the crash.)

32. FINAL EXAM

(In biology class the STUDENTS, EMILY and JENNY sit in their desks. Everyone is cramming for their test. JENNY sits silently, staring straight ahead. EMILY looks at her. PRINCIPAL SKOR enters.)

PRINCIPAL SKOR. If everyone could take out a sheet of paper and number from one to 13,

I'll be administering your test today.

JENNY. Where's …

Why isn't Mr. Christopher here?

PRINCIPAL SKOR. Mr. Christopher tendered his resignation this morning.

So

he won't be in today.

(The class reacts vocally. JENNY stands up and looks at EMILY. EMILY shakes her head.)

PRINCIPAL SKOR *(cont'd)*. Students, let's quiet down.

You'll know more when I know more.

Ms. McGrath, take your seat please.

EMILY. Jenny, I didn't say anything

PRINCIPAL SKOR. Let's focus on our test here, ladies.

Ms. McGrath.

Please.

JENNY. …

Emily?

Did you kill the senior class?

PRINCIPAL SKOR. Ms. McGrath!

JENNY. When Mrs. Christopher dropped you off at your house that day did you push the bus onto the tracks?

PRINCIPAL SKOR. …

(The other STUDENTS look for EMILY to refute. EMILY and JENNY's eyes are locked. EMILY runs out of the room. Smattered chaos. Exeunt.)

33. WALKING HOME 3

(EMILY runs home trying to beat a phone call.)

ALL. Did you hear?

No.

Did you hear?

Emily caused the bus accident.

What?

No.

No.

We need to talk.

She did it.

People are talking.

Think about it.

She moved the bus onto the tracks.

No.

That's impossible.

Somebody better call Joyce.

Emily Book killed the children.

The kids are all talking about it.

This isn't funny.

Someone should call Albert.

She used her power to move the bus.

Does Albert know?

You've seen what she can do.

Call Joyce.

34. FALLOUT

(JOYCE is waiting in Sara's room. EMILY enters.)

JOYCE. Come here, sweety.

It's OK. *(Holds EMILY.)*

Emily?

Did you kill my daughter?

(EMILY doesn't answer.)

JOYCE *(cont'd)*. Answer me.

(EMILY doesn't answer.)

JOYCE *(cont'd)*. Say it.

Say it.

EMILY. I didn't mean to.

(JOYCE gasps. She slaps EMILY.)

EMILY *(cont'd)*. I didn't know it was going to happen,

I couldn't stop it.

JOYCE. You lied.

You lied to me.

EMILY. I was scared.

JOYCE. Liar!

　You came into my home.

　And you lied!

EMILY. I …

　I'm sorry.

JOYCE. I want my daughter back!

EMILY. …

JOYCE. Can you do that?

　Can you bring her back to me?

(EMILY can't. JOYCE leaves EMILY alone.)

35. GRANDMOTHER

(EMILY remembers her last moments with her GRAND-MOTHER.)

DRIVER. Is this her?

GRANDMOTHER. Yes.

DRIVER. Hello there, Emily.

　You're grandma's told me a lot about you.

EMILY. …

DRIVER. My name is Thomas.

GRANDMOTHER. She hasn't spoken since—

DRIVER. That's OK.

GRANDMOTHER. Emily?

　Thomas is from St. Clotilde's.

　It's a wonderful place for little girls and boys—

　like you.

DRIVER. It's a very special school, Emily.

　The other children are all very excited to meet you.

EMILY. I didn't mean to do it.

DRIVER. …

   I know you didn't.

   You have nothing to worry about Emily.

EMILY. I don't want to go.

GRANDMOTHER. Emily, I love you very much,But I don't know what else to do for you.

   You have to go.

36. ESCAPE

(EMILY grabs her suitcase and climbs out the window of Sara's room.)

37. SHERIFF KNOCKING

(ALBERT enters the house.)

ALBERT. Joyce!

   (CHARLIE runs in. ALBERT holds him. JOYCE enters.)

ALBERT *(cont'd)*. Where is she?

JOYCE. …

ALBERT. Where is she, Joyce?

JOYCE. Upstairs.

   (Doorbell.)

ALBERT. Who's there?

SHERIFF. Albert, it's Louis.

   I need to speak to Emily.

ALBERT. …

SHERIFF. Albert, can you open the door?

   I just need to talk to her.

ALBERT. …

(ALBERT opens the door. SHERIFF ROSENTHAL enters, followed by other TOWNSPEOPLE. Though somewhat ashamed, everyone needs answers. ALBERT nods. He glances at JOYCE, then sets CHARLIE down by SHERIFF ROSENTHAL.)

ALBERT *(cont'd)*. Stand right here. *(Goes upstairs.)*

(After enough time has passed, ALBERT returns.)

ALBERT *(cont'd)*. She's gone.

SHERIFF ROSENTHAL. Now, Albert, I'm not here to make trouble,

I'm here to keep it from—

ALBERT. The window's open, Louis.

She's gone.

COACH ADAMS. I'll check the school.

MARK GILBERT. I'll come with you.

ALBERT. We'll help you look.

(The TOWNSPEOPLE begin their search. JOYCE and ALBERT follow.)

38. CAUGHT BY DAN

(EMILY is running. She is stopped by MR. CHRISTOPHER.)

MR. CHRISTOPHER. It's true, isn't it?

EMILY. They're looking for me.

MR. CHRISTOPHER. Where are you going?

EMILY. I don't know.

...

Mr. Christopher—

MR. CHRISTOPHER. I don't want to hear it.

EMILY. ...

MR. CHRISTOPHER. Take my ticket.

Go to Chicago.

Don't come back.

Take it!

EMILY. She was always very nice to me.

MR. CHRISTOPHER. Please leave!

(EMILY turns to go. She is blocked as the crowd arrives, blocking all the exits.)

39. STANDOFF

ALLISON MCGRATH. She's here!

MARK GILBERT. She was trying to run!

SHERIFF ROSENTHAL. Stay where you are, Emily.

(EMILY begins to fly.)

TAMMY ADAMS. Don't let her fly!

COACH ADAMS. Grab her!

SHERIFF ROSENTHAL. Bring her down!

(EMILY is restrained. She defends herself with her powers. It only takes a few moves for the standoff to become very dangerous. The crowd realizes it is caught in a stalemate.)

SHERIFF ROSENTHAL. Emily!

I don't want to hurt you.

(EMILY looks as though she might explode. And just when it seems that the conflict might be quelled with stillness, JENNY grabs SHERIFF ROSENTHAL's pistol from his holster and points it at EMILY.)

MR. CHRISTOPHER. …

Jenny,

don't.

(JENNY turns and shoots MR. CHRISTOPHER in the heart. He falls to the ground.)

40. SHOT THROUGH THE HEART

(MR. CHRISTOPHER falls to the ground, dying. The TOWNSPEOPLE do all they can to keep him alive, but realize they are helpless. EMILY steps toward JENNY and offers to take the gun from her. JENNY hands it over. EMILY carefully returns the gun to SHERIFF ROSENTHAL. She looks down at MR. CHRISTOPHER, and SHERIFF ROSENTHAL moves his attempted rescuers off, cautiously making room for EMILY. She kneels at his side. Seeping into her consciousness are the irregular beats of a muscle that is being told by the brain to pump but is physically damaged and straining to oblige. The light wheezing of lungs. Her hands become less busy on MR. CHRISTOPHER's body and eventually come to rest over the bullet hole in his sternum. The beating becomes faint. His heart beats for the last time and MR. CHRISTOPHER is frozen in death.

EMILY raises her hand a foot above MR. CHRISTOPHER's heart and closes her eyes. Her fingers and palm move in tiny and intricate ways as she remotely explores his broken heart and locates the bullet that stopped it. Then, with the center of her palm pulling, the bullet lodged in MR. CHRISTOPHER's chest extracts itself and floats towards EMILY's hand. It stops about a foot above MR. CHRISTOPHER. EMILY takes the bullet and tosses it aside. She places her hands back over his heart. With eyes closed and the deepest of concentration, EMILY repairs MR. CHRISTOPHER's heart from the inside. Leaving one hand on his heart, she uses her other to take his lifeless hand and hold it to her heart. And so, they hold each other's hearts.

Her heart beats. His heart beats. His hand returns to life and flexes against her chest. MR. CHRISTOPHER coughs. He regains his life and composure to find EMILY before him. They share a look and MR. CHRISTOPHER steps toward her. EMILY backs away.

MR. CHRISTOPHER. *The crowd. JENNY. Everyone still.)*

41. FLOAT

(EMILY picks up her suitcase, takes a look at the town and begins to walk away. She uses her power as she goes.

With a release that is not healing, forgiving, nor resolving, the town is given the gift of flight. They float amongst each other, perhaps breathing with each other and seeing one another for the first time in 10 years. Light, they float away.)

42. TRAIN RIDE

(Dawn has just started to break. EMILY rides alone, lonely, on a passenger train across Illinois. She stares blankly out her window, taking in only the experiences that brought her here.

Moments go by.

Through the reflection, over the horizon, interlaced with the golden rays of the sun, emerges the great city of Chicago.

EMILY places her hand and face against the window and looks with eyes wide to her new home.)

THE END

NOTES

NOTES

NOTES